Instant LinkedIn Customization How-to

Attract your dream job or customer using the
hidden secrets of one of the most powerful
social networking websites

Anmol Jain

PUBLISHING

BIRMINGHAM - MUMBAI

Instant LinkedIn Customization How-to

First published: February 2013

Production Reference: 1050213

Published by Packt Publishing Ltd.
Livery Place
35 Livery Street
Birmingham B3 2PB, UK.

ISBN 978-1-84969-424-7

www.packtpub.com

Credits

Author
Anmol Jain

Reviewer
Gary Saunders

Acquisition Editor
Joanna Finchen

Commissioning Editor
Meeta Rajani

Technical Editor
Prasad Dalvi

Copy Editor
Brandt D'Mello

Project Coordinators
Priya Sharma
Esha Thakker

Proofreader
Linda Morris

Production Coordinator
Prachali Bhiwandkar

Cover Work
Prachali Bhiwandkar

Cover Image
Conidon Miranda

About the Author

Anmol Jain has been studying the innovations in social networking and their impact on people over the past few years. He believes that the growing impact of social networking websites over the years will change the way people interact personally and professionally, and he is keen to share his knowledge with us.

Anmol is currently pursuing his MBA from the Hong Kong University of Science and Technology. Prior to pursuing his MBA, Anmol has worked in the advisory teams of reputed consulting companies in India and Hong Kong, such as KPMG and Ernst & Young, and provided business and IT solutions to their clients.

I would like to express my gratitude to the many people who saw me through this book, to all those who provided support, talked things over, read, wrote, offered comments, allowed me to quote their remarks, and assisted in the editing, proofreading, and design.

I would like to thank Packt Publishing and its supportive staff members Priya and Meeta for enabling me to publish this book.

I would like to thank Gary Saunders for helping me with the process of editing. Above all I would like to thank my parents and my sister who encouraged me to write this book.

About the Reviewer

Gary Saunders is a native of Australia. He has lived and worked in Australia, Europe, and Asia, and gained experience in a variety of companies ranging from FTSE 100 multinationals to Big 4 consulting firms. Working within Audit, Gary meets, interacts, and networks with a range of staff from the CEO to down. He is a keen experimenter with new technologies. He has been a member of LinkedIn since 2004.

I would like to thank Anmol for inviting me to contribute to the editing of this book and my wife Erica for her loving support.

www.PacktPub.com

Support files, eBooks, discount offers and more

You might want to visit www.PacktPub.com for support files and downloads related to your book.

Did you know that Packt offers eBook versions of every book published, with PDF and ePub files available? You can upgrade to the eBook version at www.PacktPub.com and as a print book customer, you are entitled to a discount on the eBook copy. Get in touch with us at service@packtpub.com for more details.

At www.PacktPub.com, you can also read a collection of free technical articles, sign up for a range of free newsletters and receive exclusive discounts and offers on Packt books and eBooks.

http://PacktLib.PacktPub.com

Do you need instant solutions to your IT questions? PacktLib is Packt's online digital book library. Here, you can access, read and search across Packt's entire library of books.

Why Subscribe?

- ▶ Fully searchable across every book published by Packt
- ▶ Copy and paste, print and bookmark content
- ▶ On demand and accessible via web browser

Free Access for Packt account holders

If you have an account with Packt at www.PacktPub.com, you can use this to access PacktLib today and view nine entirely free books. Simply use your login credentials for immediate access.

Table of Contents

Preface

LinkedIn is a great social media platform that helps you connect online with people, professionally. The website is very user friendly, and this book itself covers the most important tools for job seekers and professionals and offers guaranteed results. Once you learn the basics from this book, you can master and explore the areas you enjoy the most.

This book will take you through a broad range of topics on customizing your LinkedIn profile, so it's personalized to your needs and preferences.

Instant LinkedIn Customization How-to is written in such a way that each recipe is an independent new feature of LinkedIn. You can learn and apply any new concept by just reading a recipe.

You will learn customizing your profile and showcasing your work and projects to other users. Reach out to target recruiters and customers by growing your lifelong network and becoming popular. Discover different ways of finding jobs, using groups, and much more.

You will learn the art of customizing your profile and will experience networking using LinkedIn.

What this book covers

Vanity URL (Must know) explains how to create your own personalized vanity URL, which can be a potent marketing tool for your profile.

LinkedIn profile headline (Must know) illustrates how to set up your LinkedIn profile headline. Your headline is the first thing that is read about you by the other LinkedIn users, even before they get a chance to have a look at your detailed profile.

Making your profile stand out (Should know) provides you with some steps that you can perform to make your profile stand out.

Adding a video, image, document, or presentation to your profile (Should know) explains how you can display your CV and work-related presentations, videos, and so on, on your LinkedIn profile.

Messaging practically anyone with a LinkedIn account (Must know) discusses one of the most useful and powerful features of LinkedIn. In this recipe, you will learn the right approach to introducing yourself or messaging any user, before sending a connection request from your basic account.

The power of LinkedIn recommendations (Must know) explains how to write a recommendation for your colleague, mentor, student, or business partner, or to ask for one.

Taking a backup of your growing LinkedIn network (Must know) illustrates how to save the contact information for all your connections in one place.

Growing your LinkedIn network the right way (Must know) discusses how your LinkedIn connections help you develop an online network of people who may help you achieve your objective.

Steps to increase your popularity (Become an expert) discusses how to increase your popularity by active participation in a few target groups.

Sharing your LinkedIn status updates with Twitter and Facebook (Become an expert) explains how to synchronize the LinkedIn status updates with Twitter and the Twitter tweets with Facebook.

Introduction to searching for jobs on LinkedIn (Should know) explains how to look for available job openings on LinkedIn.

Equipping yourself with the advanced search skills (Become an expert) illustrates how to search for people by using the Skills & Expertise feature.

Following your target companies (Should know) discusses how to follow a company via LinkedIn.

What you need for this book

A LinkedIn account is required to perform all the recipes discussed in this book.

Who this book is for

If you're looking for a job, are genuinely interested in expanding your lifelong professional network, or simply want to learn tips and tricks for using LinkedIn, this is the right book for you.

Conventions

In this book, you will find a number of styles of text that distinguish between different kinds of information. Here are some examples of these styles, and an explanation of their meaning.

Code words in text are shown as follows: "Now, you can see a URL, for example, `http://in.linkedin.com/pub/your-name/2/772/b02`."

New terms and **important words** are shown in bold. Words that you see on the screen, in menus or dialog boxes for example, appear in the text like this: "Click on the **Edit** link adjacent to it."

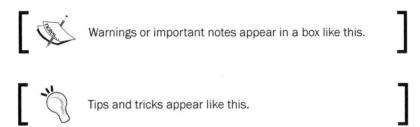

Warnings or important notes appear in a box like this.

Tips and tricks appear like this.

Reader feedback

Feedback from our readers is always welcome. Let us know what you think about this book—what you liked or may have disliked. Reader feedback is important for us to develop titles that you really get the most out of.

To send us general feedback, simply send an e-mail to feedback@packtpub.com, and mention the book title via the subject of your message.

If there is a book that you need and would like to see us publish, please send us a note in the **SUGGEST A TITLE** form on www.packtpub.com or e-mail suggest@packtpub.com.

If there is a topic that you have expertise in and you are interested in either writing or contributing to a book, see our author guide on www.packtpub.com/authors.

Customer support

Now that you are the proud owner of a Packt book, we have a number of things to help you to get the most from your purchase.

Downloading the color images of this book

We also provide you a PDF file that has color images of the screenshots/diagrams used in this book. The color images will help you better understand the changes in the output.

You can download this file from http://www.packtpub.com/sites/default/files/downloads/4247OT_ColoredImages.pdf.

Errata

Although we have taken every care to ensure the accuracy of our content, mistakes do happen. If you find a mistake in one of our books—maybe a mistake in the text or the code—we would be grateful if you would report this to us. By doing so, you can save other readers from frustration and help us improve subsequent versions of this book. If you find any errata, please report them by visiting http://www.packtpub.com/support, selecting your book, clicking on the **errata submission form** link, and entering the details of your errata. Once your errata are verified, your submission will be accepted and the errata will be uploaded on our website, or added to any list of existing errata, under the Errata section of that title. Any existing errata can be viewed by selecting your title from http://www.packtpub.com/support.

Piracy

Piracy of copyright material on the Internet is an ongoing problem across all media. At Packt, we take the protection of our copyright and licenses very seriously. If you come across any illegal copies of our works, in any form, on the Internet, please provide us with the location address or website name immediately so that we can pursue a remedy.

Please contact us at copyright@packtpub.com with a link to the suspected pirated material.

We appreciate your help in protecting our authors, and our ability to bring you valuable content.

Questions

You can contact us at questions@packtpub.com if you are having a problem with any aspect of the book, and we will do our best to address it.

Instant LinkedIn Customization How-to

Welcome to *Instant LinkedIn Customization How-to*, the book that will help you to unleash the power of the world's largest professional networking website, LinkedIn, using powerful tips and tricks.

Using the easy-to-implement LinkedIn customizations that you will learn in this book, you can:

- ▸ Expand your professional network
- ▸ Start your dream career
- ▸ Attract your target business partners and customers

In the beginning

If you have been using LinkedIn and not getting the right results, or you simply want to learn some interesting and powerful features of LinkedIn to help you to grow professionally, this is the right book for you.

 The customizations introduced in this book are easy to learn and implement. However, it is assumed that you have already created a free basic LinkedIn account and have fundamental knowledge of Internet and computer usage.

Vanity URL (Must know)

Just like any other website, LinkedIn provides you with the option of creating your own personalized vanity URL, which can be a potent marketing tool for your profile.

How to do it...

To set your own personalized vanity URL, perform the following steps:

1. Firstly, click on the **Edit Profile** button via the LinkedIn toolbar located at the top of your page, which appears after you log in:

2. You will now see a URL, for example, `http://in.linkedin.com/pub/your-name/2/772/b02`. Click on the **Edit** link adjacent to it.

3. You will now see a section titled **Your Public Profile URL** on the right-hand side of the page. Click on **Customize your public profile URL**.

4. Now, enter your custom URL closest to your first or last name, depending on the availability, and click on the **Set Custom URL** button:

Your vanity URL is now set.

You can also obtain your personalized button, known as a **profile badge**, to promote your profile on other websites.

1. When you click on **Customize your public profile URL**, as explained earlier, you will see a button called **Create a profile badge** in the same section. Click on it.

2. Now, you will see different style buttons with the corresponding source code, which you can copy to your website or blog to promote your LinkedIn profile page:

How it works...

Now that you have set your vanity URL, as explained in the preceding section, your LinkedIn profile will have become more search engine friendly.

There's more...

Apart from just setting up your vanity URL, you can perform some of the following tasks to maximize the use of your vanity URL:

▶ Promote your URL and profile badge by sharing them on your website or blog.

▶ Share your URL and profile badge with your friends and colleagues. One of the easiest ways to do this is to put it in your e-mail signature.

▶ Get your URL printed on your business card.

 LinkedIn has more than 100 million registered users. Simple steps, such as printing your vanity URL on business cards can help you to expand your professional network exponentially.

LinkedIn profile headline (Must know)

Every LinkedIn user can customize his/her profile headline. Your headline is the first thing that is read about you by other LinkedIn users, even before they get a chance to have a look at your detailed profile. Hence, this tool should be used wisely so that it can attract the right audience.

The following screenshot shows what a profile headline looks like:

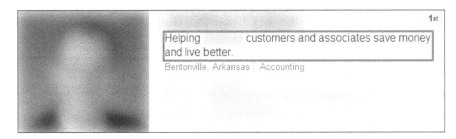

How to do it...

To set up your LinkedIn profile headline, perform the following steps:

1. Click on the **Edit Profile** button from the LinkedIn toolbar located at the top of the page that appears after you log in.

2. Click on the button located next to your current headline, and you will see a screen, as shown in the following screenshot:

3. Input the professional headline for the target audience.

How it works...

You've now learned how to update your LinkedIn profile headline. The key point is to be as specific as you can and put the right keywords that are search engine friendly and eye catching. Let me state a few examples:

- **Job seeker headline**:

  5 years of exp in Java and .NET; looking for opportunities in Hong Kong

- **Service marketing headline**:

  Helping fortune 500 companies increase revenues by designing better HR strategies

- **Examples of a few other interesting headlines**:

  - Chief Operating Officer; building high performing sales teams that align with corporate vision

  - Experienced sales professional looking to positively impact a new organization

  - Retail technology solutions; developing high performing retail outlets

 It is a good idea to refine and update your profile headline regularly, so that your profile is viewed by the right audience.

Making your profile stand out (Should know)

Your LinkedIn profile should be a reflection of your resume. It is a good idea to provide as much relevant information about your qualifications and experience as possible. LinkedIn itself is a very friendly networking website and prompts you about the completion status of your profile, on the right-hand side of the page, when you click on the **View Profile** button on the toolbar:

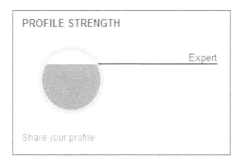

You can complete your profile by using the **Improve your profile** button and achieve an **All Star** status, which means that your profile is 100 percent complete.

There are a few optional sections that could be added to your profile depending upon your qualifications and experience:

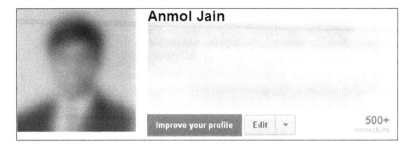

How to do it...

Here are some steps that you can perform to make your profile stand out:

1. Click on **Edit Profile** from the LinkedIn toolbar located at the top of the page that appears after you log in.

2. You will see a **Recommended for you** section in the top-right corner of the page. You can add many more relevant sections, including **PROJECTS**, **PUBLICATIONS**, **TEST SCORES**, and so on, to further enhance your profile for the target audience:

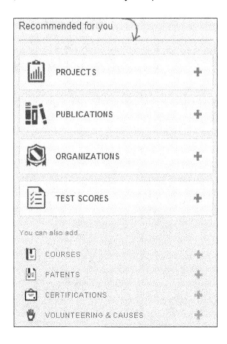

3. Apart from these sections, you can also display your work, CV, videos, and so on, by associating links with your profile. We will have a look at this in the forthcoming recipe.

How it works...

By adding sections to your profile, you can provide more information about yourself to the target audience and hence make your profile stand out.

[Please devote some time to completing your Linkedin profile to the best of your knowledge. Providing the right keywords throughout your profile will help you reach out to the target audience much faster.]

Adding a video, image, document, or presentation to your profile (Should know)

LinkedIn does not host files directly. However, it allows you to upload links in the relevant sections of your profile, where you can display your CV and work-related presentations, videos, and documents. This is a great tool to give out more information about yourself and distinguish yourself from other users.

How to do it...

To add a video, image, document, or presentation, perform the following steps:

1. Click on the **Edit Profile** button from the LinkedIn toolbar located at the top of the page that appears after you log in.

2. Scroll down to the related section and click on the square icon to display your work on your LinkedIn profile:

3. Provide a link to the source page and press *Enter*. The link to your file will get associated with your profile page.

How it works...

You have now successfully learned how to display your work on your LinkedIn profile from external sources.

Please note that LinkedIn previously used to have a dedicated section called **Applications**, where you could integrate third-party applications with your profile. Some of the applications were Poll, Box.Net Files, Slide Share Presentations, BlogLink, and so on. This feature has since been discontinued for simplicity. However, you can still host your files on these websites and provide a link to them, as explained in the preceding *How to do it...* section.

 Adding your CV to your LinkedIn profile gives better accessibility to recruiters, company HR, and business partners. Keep updating your CV regularly for targeted results.

There's more...

Apart from sharing your work on your profile, it is also important to share links to your blog, company, or personal websites that will be visible in the **Contact Info** section of your profile.

You can do the same by clicking on **Edit Contact Info** and then editing the websites section by using the pencil icon, as shown in the following screenshot:

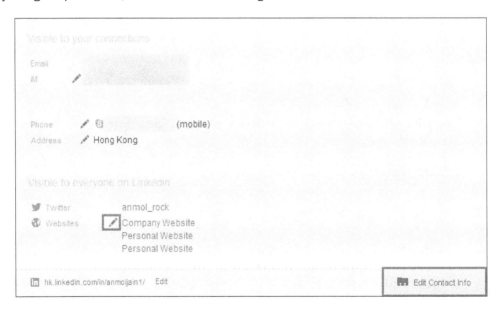

Messaging practically anyone with a LinkedIn account (Must know)

In this section, we will discuss one of the most useful and powerful features of LinkedIn. You may sometimes want to send a message to a recruiter or a potential business partner. However, the website does not allow us to send a message to a user without adding him as your connection. Also, you cannot send an **Add Connection** request to just any person because that might result in **I don't Know** responses and restrictions to your account. So, what would be the right approach to introduce yourself to, or message, any user before sending a connection request from your basic account? The answer is by joining the same interest group as the person you're interested in connecting with.

How to do it...

To start, let's assume that you want to send a message to me, Anmol Jain, as connecting with me can help your business or get you a job. However, we don't have any common connections. The following is the approach you can take:

1. You can view my profile page and scroll down to the **GROUPS** section, as shown in the following screenshot. You can now see all the groups that I'm a member of:

2. Click on an appropriate group that you are also interested in. You will now be taken to the group's home page. Click on the **Join Group** button, as shown in the following screenshot:

3. Depending upon the type of group, your request will be accepted. For an open group, you don't need administrator approval and you can join immediately. For a closed group, your request will be accepted depending upon the group administrator's response, and this usually takes one or two days.

   However, please do not join just any group. For example, if you are not an alumnus of a university, the group administrator might not accept your request.

   Once you are a member of a group, you will see a new **Members** tab, as shown in the following screenshot:

4. Click on the **Members** tab and enter the name of the person you're searching for; enter Anmol Jain, in this case:

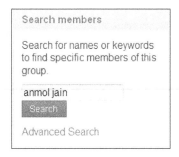

5. You will find the person in **Search Results**, as demonstrated in the following screenshot:

   Now, using the **Send message** button on the right-hand side, you can send a direct message or your introduction to me without adding me as a connection.

How it works...

What's so special about this feature? Using this method, you can send a message to almost every person on LinkedIn, because each LinkedIn member is usually a member of at least one group. However, this feature should be used with care, because otherwise this might be perceived as spamming and your account might get restricted.

Unlike the **Connection Request** text, when you're sending a direct message to a person, you can send a much longer message. It is recommended that you introduce yourself, clearly state your objective, and suggest the next steps when messaging the target person.

> When looking for a job, think of the person who would be in the best position to hire you before connecting with him. For example, if you are looking for a job as a consultant in a management consulting firm, you might want to search for a manager.

The power of LinkedIn recommendations (Must know)

Recommendations is a basic feature of LinkedIn. You can write a recommendation for your colleague, mentor, student, or business partner, or you can ask for one. The number of recommendations that you've received and the recommendation texts are visible on your profile.

Even though you may already know how to write or request a recommendation, let us still have a quick look at how to do this, before learning some useful tips and tricks at the end of this chapter.

How to do it...

Let us learn how to receive a recommendation:

1. Click on **Recommendations** under the **Profile** tab of the LinkedIn toolbar.

2. You will see three tabs on the following screen. To request a recommendation, click on the **Request Recommendations** tab:

Received Recommendations	Sent Recommendations	Request Recommendations

3. Select the job role or school for which you are seeking recommendation and the person whom you are requesting the recommendation from.

4. Write a personalized recommendation request and your message will be sent. You will be notified via an e-mail or via the **Messages** section within your LinkedIn account once the person writes a recommendation for you. You can then choose to accept or reject it:

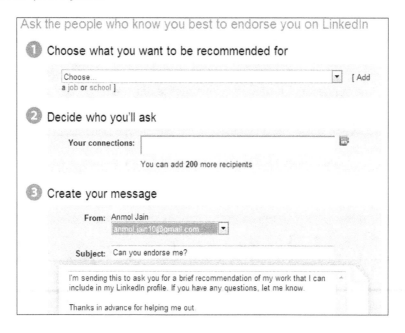

Let us learn how to write a recommendation:

1. To recommend a person, you need to visit the profile page of the connection and click on the **Recommend** button located under the **Send a message** button on his/her profile page, as shown in the following screenshot:

2. Now select the type of relationship, the basis of recommendation, and write a brief recommendation. Your recommendation will be sent and will be visible on the profile of the person you recommend, with your name included.

Let us learn how to endorse our connections for their skills:

1. LinkedIn has recently added a new feature that allows you to endorse your connections for their skills. Unlike the recommendations, endorsements are just one click away. The more endorsements you give, the more likely you are to receive them since they are just a click away. Hence, it is also important to fill your **SKILLS & EXPERTISE** section as accurately as possible.

2. To endorse a person, you need to visit the profile page of the connection and scroll down to the **SKILLS & EXPERTISE** section.

3. Click on the **+** button located next to the skill that you would like to endorse; the same will be visible on your connections' profile page:

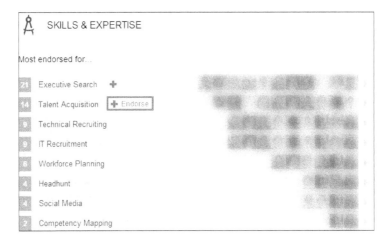

How it works...

You've just learnt how to send and receive recommendations to and from your connections. However, it is important to learn how to identify the right people to approach for writing a recommendation and how many recommendations should be good to attract the target audience. The answer lies in the following section.

There's more...

During the hiring process, most companies ask you to provide contact details of one or two colleagues or supervisors from your past employer. Recommendations on your profile reflect the authenticity of your work. So why not integrate this crucial aspect of hiring on your profile. On LinkedIn, there is no limit to the number of recommendations you can obtain.

The most important question is, "Is it the number of recommendations that matter or the position of the recommender?"

The number of recommendations on your profile definitely catches the eye of recruiters and potential business partners, but it will not assure results. Every recommendation that you receive should uncover a unique trait or characteristic of your work. It should be from a diverse set of colleagues, classmates, mentors, and business partners. It will not be a good idea to receive five recommendations from your friends in your class or a colleague at the same level. That would surely make it look dubious, even though it is 100 percent authentic.

Let's consider that I am a graduate from the Hong Kong University of Science and Technology. I have worked with two companies, KPMG and Ernst & Young, in a management consulting role. Assuming my tenure has been 1 year in the first company and 2 years in the second, I would aim to have the following recommendations on my profile:

▶ Two recommendations from mentors at the University

▶ Two recommendations from classmates and friends

▶ One recommendation from a manager at KPMG

▶ One recommendation from a colleague at KPMG

▶ One recommendation from a manager at Ernst & Young

▶ Two recommendations from supervisors at Ernst & Young (assuming that I have at least two supervisors and one manager at the company)

▶ Two recommendation from juniors at Ernst & Young (assuming that I manage at least two people at the company)

The preceding list is just an estimate of how you should balance the recommendations on your LinkedIn profile. It may vary from person to person, depending upon your education, experience, and extracurricular work.

 While obtaining recommendations, keep in mind that legitimacy, diversity, and quality speak louder than anything else.

Taking a backup of your growing LinkedIn network (Must know)

You've worked hard to grow your LinkedIn network. Now, it's your responsibility to save the contact information of all your connections in one place, no matter what happens to your LinkedIn account. Moreover, you might want to save the data of all your connections in a directory or in an e-mail client such as Microsoft Outlook to reach out to them faster. Fortunately, LinkedIn provides this feature just through a single click.

How to do it...

To back up your growing LinkedIn network, perform the following steps:

1. Click on **Connections** on the **Contacts** tab on the LinkedIn toolbar.

2. You will see a list of all your connections. At the bottom-right corner of the page, you will see a link **Export connections**, as shown in the following screenshot. Click on it:

147 outstanding sent invitations | Export connections |

3. Select the type of file format in which you want to export the connections and click on the **Export** button:

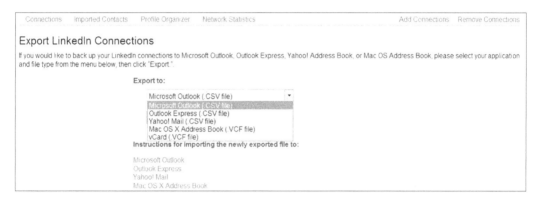

How it works...

You have just learned how to back up your valuable LinkedIn network. Reaching out to your connections just got easier. You have all the contact details of your connections at one place.

 Back up your LinkedIn connections once a month. This will insure you against virus attacks, and you never know when this feature may be removed by LinkedIn.

Growing your LinkedIn network the right way (Must know)

In real life, the people you know as relatives, friends, or colleagues act as catalysts to help you find the right job or that perfect business opportunity. Your LinkedIn connections help you develop an online network of people to help you achieve the same objective.

The following are some of the reasons why expanding your network is essential to your career:

- ▸ Once your network has reached a certain number of connections, it goes into autopilot mode and keeps growing automatically. By autopilot, I mean that you will start receiving many more connection requests than usual.

- ▸ You can access contact details such as e-mail addresses, phone numbers, and mailing addresses when you add people to your network.

- ▸ When you have a large number of connections in your network, you enter the active member list of a LinkedIn search and your profile is more likely to be among the top few searches, even if there are many people with your name.

- ▸ When you log in to your LinkedIn account, you can go to the **All Updates** tab, where you get the latest updates about all your connections and their networks, job postings, status updates, groups joined, and so on. It's just like following a user's profile on twitter, as shown in the following screenshot:

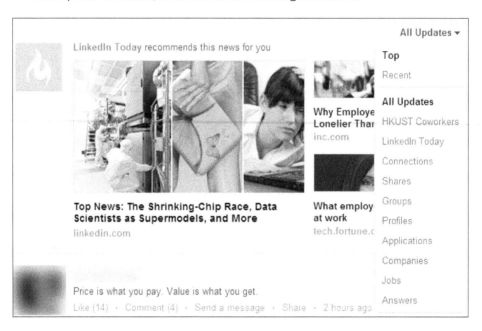

- ▸ You have better access to second-degree connections, which means more people will be willing to accept your connection request than if you had a smaller network.

- ▸ In this fast-paced world, you never know when a person leaves a company and advances his career to your target job profile. Hence, you always have a reason to add more people to your network.

To start with, it is a good idea to grow your network by adding your current colleagues, ex-colleagues, classmates, teachers, business partners, and professional acquaintances to your network. It is also a good idea to join the groups of your graduate university and all the employers you've worked with. Apart from these, the following are some of the ways you can use to swiftly expand your network:

- ► The **People You May Know** feature
- ► The **Adding relevant people using the introduction** feature
- ► Adding job consultants to your network
- ► Adding **LinkedIn Open Networkers** (**LIONs**) to your network

How to do it...

Let's learn how you can grow your network with the **People You May Know** feature:

1. Depending upon the profile information you have added, groups you've joined, schools you have attended, companies you have worked for, the kind of work you have done, and the type of connections you have, LinkedIn suggests people to add to your network by using the **People You May Know** feature.

2. You can locate the **People You May Know** box on the top-right corner of your home page, as shown in the following screenshot:

3.   Now click on **See more**. You will see the list of universities that either you are an alumnus of or are currently studying in, and of companies you have worked / are working with, as entered in your profile information. You will also see a list of those universities or companies that you follow or have most connections with, followed by the suggested people:

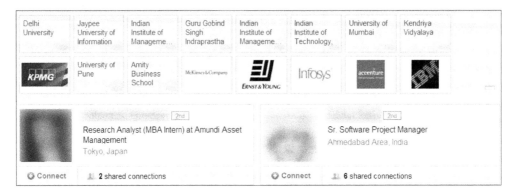

4.   If you are interested in adding people of a specific university or a company, you can filter them by clicking on that company or university, if needed. Let's select **Delhi University** as an example:

5.   Now, you can connect to the suggested connections by using the **Connect** or **Connect All** button and sending a personalized message to the people you know. However, please be cautious when using **Connect All**, because this might lead to many **I don't Know** responses from people you don't know.

Let's learn how you can grow your network by adding valuable people using the Introduction feature.

LinkedIn provides a powerful feature called **Introduction**. While sending a connection request to a second-degree connection, you can choose to be introduced by the common connection. This adds credibility to your request and increases the chances of your being accepted as a connection.

1. When you visit the profile of the person you want to add to your network, you will see a **Get introduced** link under the **Send InMail** button, as shown in the following screenshot. Click on it:

2. You will see a list of common connections. Select the appropriate common connection from which you would like help getting introduced to the person you want to add to your network:

3. Write a personalized message, which will be sent to your connection and be forwarded to the target:

Let's learn how you can grow your network by adding job consultants.

One of the easiest and most effective ways of expanding your LinkedIn network is to add job consultants, for the following reasons:

►   Job consultants will almost certainly accept your invitation because they are on a constant lookout for candidates to expand their database and to make their search easier.

►   Once you add job consultants, you will be posted on any new vacancy that arises by following their status updates. Most consultants regularly post updates about vacancies.

►   Once you have a certain number of job consultants in your network, a lot of HR personnel and consultants will keep on adding you to their networks, and you might start getting job offers from employers or consultants.

Let's assume that you are looking to build a career in Information Technology in India. The following is the approach you could follow:

1. Select **Search Companies** from the **Companies** tab located on the LinkedIn toolbar. Now, again select the **Search Companies** tab on the resultant page, as shown in the following screenshot:

2. Now, filter **Location** as **India** (select city if you need to be more specific) and **Industry** as **Human Resources** and **Staffing and Recruiting**:

3. Sort the search results by **Followers**:

4. From the search results, open the company's page and visit employee profiles. Keep adding filters. In this case, you can add IT, Software Development, Programmer, and so on in the search box. The consultants who you feel handle these types of profiles could be added to your network. You can add a few helpful consultants to your network from every company, and this can significantly grow your network and at the same time boost your job search efforts.

5. Another good aspect of adding recruitment consultants to your network is that you are able to connect to other individuals who are working in your area of interest. This is because recruitment consultants would definitely have their target candidates as their connections.

Let's learn how you can grow your network by adding LIONs.

LIONs are people who, like you, are in the process of growing their networks and would certainly accept your connection request. You can identify these people with some phrases such as LION, open networker, accept all connections, and so on in their names or profile headlines; send them connection requests. You can also add these keywords to your profile to boost receiving connection requests. You can locate these people from one of the following ways:

▸ You can search people by using the right keywords:

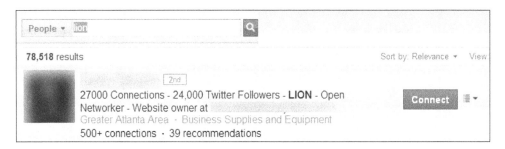

▸ You can join relevant groups on LinkedIn that are specifically created for LIONs, such as TopLinked.com, FastTrack Business Network (LION), and Leading International Open Networkers (LION).

How it works...

You've just learnt how to follow some of the techniques to grow your network faster. However, LinkedIn follows a strict anti-spam policy, so make sure you approach the right people in the right way and keep exploring your own ways to expand your network.

Using any of the methods explained in the preceding section, try to add mostly those people to your network who you think have a profile that is connected to the areas you want to work in or you want to do business in.

Steps to increase your popularity (Become an expert)

In the previous recipe, we looked at a few ways that you can expand your network. We will now look at a few ways to increase your popularity. Once you become popular on LinkedIn, you will automatically gain credibility, and your relationship with your connections will improve significantly.

There are ways by which you can popularize yourself, and one of them is active participation in a few target groups.

How to do it...

In this section, we will discuss how to increase your popularity by active participation in a few target groups.

LinkedIn has a number of corporate, university, and interest groups of which you can become a member. Apart from the corporate and university groups, which I assume you would already be a member of, identify a few interest groups (the number is up to you) and participate in them on a regular basis. This would also showcase your commitment and knowledge to the members of the group. By participation, I mean that you can either help the other members of the group by sharing your knowledge, latest news, or relevant articles, or by answering the queries of other members. Let's understand this with an example.

1. Let's consider that you have identified five interest groups to participate regularly in. One of the groups is **Global Diversity and Inclusion in the Workplace**.

2. You can ask a question, share an article, and share your own knowledge or opinion about the subject, as shown in the following screenshot:

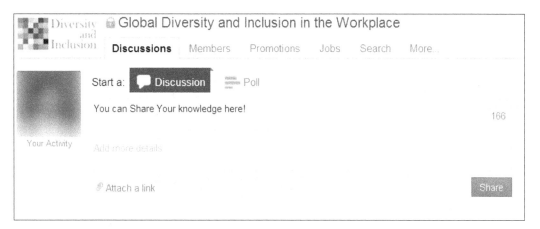

3. You can also answer a query or give your comments on the posts of other group members, as shown in the following screenshot:

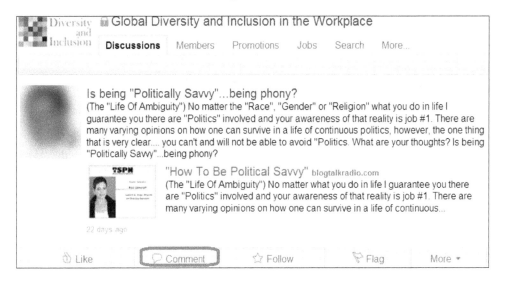

 Once you identify your target interest groups, make it a point to contribute towards each group page at least twice a week.

Now, we will discuss how to increase your popularity by using the Answers feature.

LinkedIn has come up with an interesting feature known as **Answers**. Using this feature, you can ask questions of your connections and the public and also attempt to answer questions in your area of expertise, as follows:

1. Click on **Answers** on the **More** tab on the LinkedIn toolbar:

2. You can now ask a question, as shown in the following screenshot:

Answers Home	Advanced Answers Search	My Q&A	Ask a Question	Answer Questions

Ask a Question

Thousands of professionals are available to give you an answer

Next

Answer Questions

Recommended categories for you:

* Freelancing and Contracting
* Search Marketing
* Ethics
* Starting Up
* Using LinkedIn

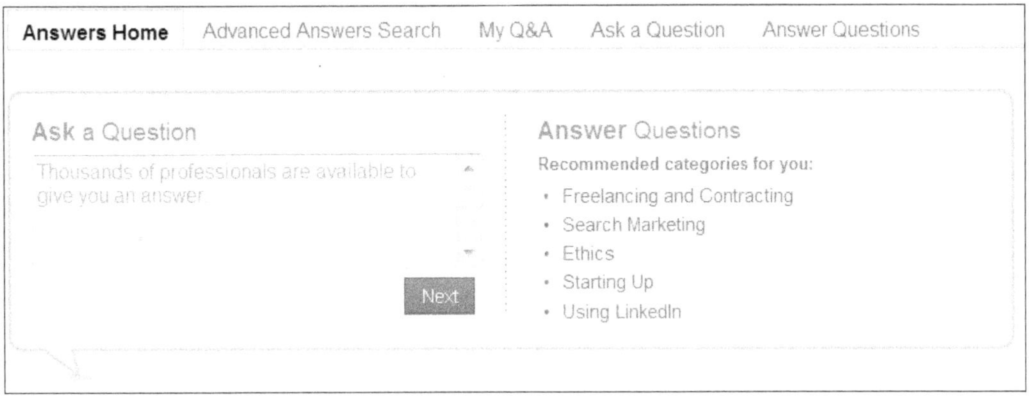

3. After clicking on **Next**, add details to your question and categorize your question. If you are interested in asking questions of only your connections, check the box shown in the following screenshot, or else your question will be posted to the public:

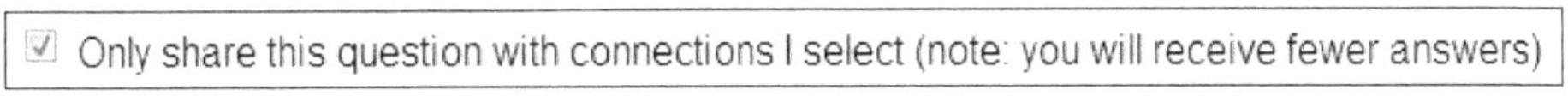

☑ Only share this question with connections I select (note: you will receive fewer answers)

4. Now you can send the question to at most 200 connections. Note that by using this feature you can reach out to 200 connections at once. However, if you send a direct message by using the **Inbox** tab on the LinkedIn toolbar, you can send a message to only 50 connections.

5. To answer a question, it is advisable that you first browse through **New Questions From Your Network**, which is located on the **Answers** home page:

New Questions From Your Network

? Do you know how I can locate hotel properties in major US urban markets that might be available for sale?
  2 answers | Asked by   [2nd] | 50 minutes ago in Mergers and Acquisitions, Corporate Debt

? I've done an advanced search in LinkedIn and I want to export the results to a .csv file.
  2 answers | Asked by   [2nd] | 3 hours ago in Using LinkedIn

6. If you don't find a relevant question, browse and select through the list of areas located on the right-hand side of the page, and then select a question to answer.

Now, we will discuss how to increase your popularity by sharing status updates regularly.

Just like Twitter and Facebook, where we share everything about our lives with our followers, we can use the LinkedIn status updates to share what's happening in our professional lives. We can share news and article links, blog links, or updates about our work or projects. It is a good idea to regularly share updates so that you frequently appear in the eyes of your connections.

On your LinkedIn home page, you will see the following box to share an update:

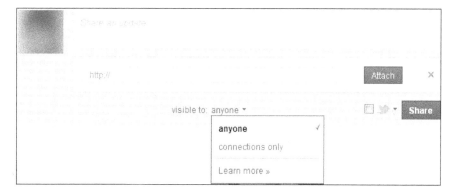

How it works...

The steps discussed in the preceding section will help you to gain credibility on LinkedIn and on the web. Slowly, you will be able to strengthen your network and leverage its potential in real life.

The type of groups you join, the type of questions you answer, and the type of status updates you share all determine the type of people you attract towards your network, so please use them carefully.

Sharing your LinkedIn status updates with Twitter and Facebook (Become an expert)

The three most popular social networking websites as of today are LinkedIn, Facebook, and Twitter. Sharing your LinkedIn status updates with the other two websites can help you spread the status updates with a simple setting, and the message is easily spread to more people. Let's learn how to do it.

How to do it...

Firstly, let's learn how to synchronize the LinkedIn status updates with Twitter:

1. Click on the **Edit Profile** button from the **Profile** tab on the LinkedIn toolbar.

2. Click on the **Edit Contact Info** button. You will see a **Twitter** section, where you can link a Twitter account:

3. Once you click on **Add a Twitter account**, a window will open up asking you to enter your Twitter credentials and ask for app authorization:

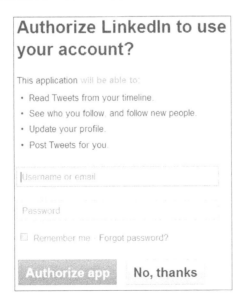

4. Your LinkedIn and Twitter accounts are now linked. All your LinkedIn status updates will be shown on Twitter tweets provided that you check the Twitter checkbox located on the bottom-right corner of the status update box, as shown in the following screenshot:

Now, let's learn how to synchronize the Twitter tweets with Facebook.

Your LinkedIn status updates cannot be directly synchronized with Facebook. Hence, you need to synchronize your Twitter tweets with Facebook status updates; this will indirectly update your LinkedIn status updates to Facebook.

1. Log in to your Twitter account and click on **Settings** on the drop-down menu located at the top-right corner of the page.
2. Select the **Profile** tab from the **Setting** menu options now available.
3. At the bottom of the page, you will see the button shown in the following screenshot. Click on it:

4. You will be asked to enter your Facebook credentials and authorize Twitter to access your Facebook account:

How it works...

The steps discussed in the preceding section will help you to share your professional LinkedIn status updates with Twitter and Facebook.

You don't need to share all your LinkedIn status updates with Twitter and Facebook. It is recommended that you share only those updates that need to reach out to a much larger audience and could be shared with your Twitter followers and Facebook friends.

Introduction to searching for jobs on LinkedIn (Should know)

Many of the recipes discussed in this book are somehow related to finding jobs indirectly. However, let's see some of the steps you can follow to search and apply for jobs directly. This can be done by either finding jobs through direct search or browsing through the **Jobs** section in some groups.

How to do it...

Let's learn how to find jobs through direct search:

1. Click on the **Find Jobs** section from the **Jobs** tab on the LinkedIn toolbar.

2. Based on your profile information, a few jobs will be suggested to you, to which you can apply.

3. You can also do a basic or advanced search. Using the **Advanced Search** option, you can filter the job search on the basis of keywords, location, country, job title, company, functions, experience, industries, date posted, and salary.

Most head-hunters regularly post updates about job openings through status updates. Hence, you should keep an eye on the status updates visible on your home page.

Let's learn how to browse through the **Jobs** section in some groups:

1. Go to the interest group in the area you are looking for jobs. Some groups have a **Jobs** section in a separate tab, as shown in the following screenshot. Click on it:

2. On the left-hand side of the page, you will be able to see two links—**Jobs** and **Job Discussions**.

3. **Jobs** basically shows all the relevant LinkedIn jobs that are shared by the members of the group, as shown in the following screenshot:

4. The **Job Discussions** section is generally a discussion about jobs that might include external job links, suggestions for jobs, and so on:

How it works...

You've just learnt some of the direct ways to look for available job openings on LinkedIn.

Equipping yourself with the advanced search skills (Become an expert)

Searching for the right people on LinkedIn can be a challenge sometimes. It would be good to know some simple tips on how you can locate your target audience in easier and faster ways. You can search for people by using the **Skills & Expertise** feature, apart from using the **Advanced Search** feature.

How to do it...

Let's learn how to search for people by using **Skills & Expertise**:

1. LinkedIn provides a feature that allows you to narrow down your search. Click on **Skills & Expertise** from the **More** dropdown on the LinkedIn toolbar.

2. Now you need to enter the type of skills your target audience should possess. Let's suppose you enter **Management Consulting**, the following screen will appear:

3. Related to that skill, you will be able to find related skills, find groups and jobs for those skills, find companies that employ such skills, and so on. All this information will be extremely useful in your search.

How it works...

The steps discussed in the preceding section will help you to find your target audience faster.

Please note, that LinkedIn offers many search filters when searching for people or companies. Please use these features to their full potential. For example, you can filter people to search by companies, relationship, location, industry, and school.

Following your target companies (Should know)

We are always looking for companies either to find work or to find clients. With LinkedIn, it's easier to keep a track of your target companies. Once you identify your prospective clients, customers, or employers, you can start following these companies and be updated about their latest news, insights, and career updates.

How to do it...

To follow a company, perform the following steps:

1. To follow a company, all you need to do is to search for the company and click on the **Follow** button, as shown in the following screenshot:

2. On the company's page, you will see four tabs—**Home**, **Careers**, **Products & Services**, and **Insights**.

   ❑ **Home**: This tab provides you with brief information and updates about your network in that company

   ❑ **Careers**: This tab provides information about job openings, employee reviews, and HR contacts

   ❑ **Products & Services**: This tab provides information about company products and services, and any updates on them

   ❑ **Insights**: This tab provides information about new hires, departures, connection graphs, most popular company locations, and most common skills of the employees

How it works...

As LinkedIn regularly updates its website and company pages, it is becoming more important to follow your target companies to find your dream job or acquire a new customer. You can learn about all the latest happenings in the company. This would definitely help you in the near future.

 Do not follow hundreds of companies. It would be a good idea to follow fewer companies and stay focused on them for job openings, news updates, and latest trends.

There's more...

Apart from following the companies, you should also be updated about the latest news in the functions and industries relevant to you by using the **News** section located on the LinkedIn toolbar.

LinkedIn has also introduced a new feature where you can follow the world's leading influencers and thought leaders at `http://www.linkedin.com/today/post/whoToFollow`.

 **Thank you for buying**
Instant LinkedIn Customization How-to

About Packt Publishing

Packt, pronounced 'packed', published its first book "*Mastering phpMyAdmin for Effective MySQL Management*" in April 2004 and subsequently continued to specialize in publishing highly focused books on specific technologies and solutions.

Our books and publications share the experiences of your fellow IT professionals in adapting and customizing today's systems, applications, and frameworks. Our solution based books give you the knowledge and power to customize the software and technologies you're using to get the job done. Packt books are more specific and less general than the IT books you have seen in the past. Our unique business model allows us to bring you more focused information, giving you more of what you need to know, and less of what you don't.

Packt is a modern, yet unique publishing company, which focuses on producing quality, cutting-edge books for communities of developers, administrators, and newbies alike. For more information, please visit our website: www.packtpub.com.

Writing for Packt

We welcome all inquiries from people who are interested in authoring. Book proposals should be sent to author@packtpub.com. If your book idea is still at an early stage and you would like to discuss it first before writing a formal book proposal, contact us; one of our commissioning editors will get in touch with you.

We're not just looking for published authors; if you have strong technical skills but no writing experience, our experienced editors can help you develop a writing career, or simply get some additional reward for your expertise.

ASP.NET 4 Social Networking

ISBN: 978-1-84969-082-9   Paperback: 484 pages

A truly hands-on book for ASP.NET 4 Developers

1. Create a full-featured, enterprise-grade social network using ASP.NET 4.0

2. Learn key new ASP.NET and .NET Framework concepts like Managed Extensibility Framework (MEF), Entity Framework 4.0, LINQ, AJAX, C# 4.0, ASP.NET Routing,n-tier architectures, and MVP in a practical, hands-on way.

3. Build friends lists, messaging systems, user profiles, blogs, forums, groups, and more

4. A practical guide full of step by step explanations, interesting examples, and practical advice

Facebook Application Development with Graph API Cookbook

ISBN: 978-1-84969-092-8   Paperback: 350 pages

Over 90 recipes to create your own exciting Facebook applications at an incredibly fast pace with facebook Graph API

1. Dive headfirst into Facebook application development with the all new Facebook Graph API.

2. Packed with many demonstrations on how to use Facebook PHP and JS SDKs.

3. Step by step examples demonstrating common scenarios and problems encountered during Facebook Application Development.

4. Houses an exquisite collection of ready to use Facebook applications.

Please check **www.PacktPub.com** for information on our titles

PUBLISHING

HTML5 Video How-To

HTML5 Video How-To

Over 20 practical, hands-on recipes to encode and
display videos in the HTML5 video standard

Alex Libby

[PACKT]

ISBN: 978-1-84969-364-6   Paperback: 80 pages

Over 20 practical, hands-on recipes to encode and
display videos in the HTML5 video standard

1. Learn something new in an Instant! A short, fast,
    focused guide delivering immediate results.

2. Encode and embed videos into web pages using
    the HTML5 video standard

3. Publish videos to popular sites, such as YouTube
    or VideoBin

4. Provide cross-browser support for HTML5 videos
    and create your own custom video player using
    jQuery

open source
community experience distilled

FreeCAD [How-to]

Solid Modeling with the power of Python

Foreword by Yorik van Havre, FreeCAD developer

Brad Collette   Daniel Falck

[PACKT]*

FreeCAD [How-to]

ISBN: 978-1-84951-886-4   Paperback: 68 pages

Solid Modeling with the power of Python

1. Learn something new in an Instant! A short, fast,
    focused guide delivering immediate results.

2. Packed with simple and interesting examples of
    python coding for the CAD world.

3. Understand FreeCAD's approach to modeling and
    see how Python puts unprecedented power in the
    hands of users.

4. Dive into FreeCAD and its underlying scripting
    language.

Please check **www.PacktPub.com** for information on our titles